Comptroller of the Currency
Administrator of National Banks

Foreign Exchange

Comptroller's Handbook
(Section 813)

Narrative and Procedures - March 1990

Other Income Producing Activities

Foreign Exchange
(Section 813)

Table of Contents

Foreign Exchange
(Section 813)
Introduction

This section is intended to provide minimum background and procedural guidelines to examiners responsible for evaluating a bank's foreign currency activities. Within individual banks, foreign currency money market and exchange trading operations may be combined or completely separate with regard to policies, procedures, reporting, and even dealing. However, they ultimately must be viewed together to evaluate liquidity and to insure compliance with overall bank objectives and risk management strategy. For the sake of brevity, this section discusses both functions as if they were performed by the same traders, processed by the same bookkeepers and managed by the same officers. Close coordination is required among examiners performing the foreign exchange, due from banks—time, nostro account, and funds management functions.

Most importers, exporters, manufacturers, and retailers tend to let banks handle their foreign exchange needs. They rely on banks to make and receive their foreign currency payments, to provide them with foreign currency loans, to fund their foreign currency bank accounts, and to purchase their excess foreign currency balances. They may ask banks to provide such services for immediate delivery, i.e., at spot (short-term contracts, perhaps up to 10 days), or they might contract to buy or sell a specified amount of foreign currency for delivery at a future date. In either instance, the rates for such services may be established prior to the finalization of the commercial transactions, and the related costs may be calculated and often passed on to the buyers.

Risks

In contracting to meet a customer's foreign currency needs, by granting loans, accepting deposits, or providing spot or forward exchange, a bank undertakes a risk that exchange rates might change subsequent to the time the contract is made. The bank, therefore, must turn to wholesale markets, principally other banks, to acquire the cover necessary to protect itself against loss on such contracts. The astute banker manages that risk by maintaining constant surveillance over the following:

Net Open Positions. A bank has a net position in a foreign currency when its assets, including spot and future contracts to purchase, and its liabilities, including spot and future contracts to sell, in that currency are not equal. An excess of assets over liabilities is called a net "long" position and liabilities in excess of assets, a net "short" position. A long position in a currency which is depreciating will result in an exchange loss relative to book value because, with each day, that position (asset) is convertible into fewer units of local currency. Similarly, a short position in a currency that is appreciating represents an exchange loss relative to book value because, with each day, satisfaction of that position (liability) will cost more units of local currency. (Examples of net open position schedules appropriate for use in preparing the report of examination appear below.)

Consolidated Foreign Exchange Position
May 4, 19XX
(amounts in thousands)

	Assets/Purchases		Liabilities/Sales	
Monetary Unit, Overnight Limit and Description	Foreign Amount	U.S. $ Equivalent of Local Currency Book Value	Foreign Amount	U.S. $ Equivalent of Local Currency Book Value
Deutschemark ($3,000M)				
Ledger Accounts	563,437	239,461	645,013	274,310
Spot Contracts	23,502	9,802	15,973	6,709
Forward Contracts	790,250	331,905	712,533	296,342
Financial Swaps (a)	239,912	100,097	246,131	104,977
	1,617,101	681,265	1,619,650	682,338
Net Position (short)			2,549	1,073
Canadian Dollars ($6,000M)				
Ledger Accounts	1,016,076	1,017,525	1,029,835	1,030,057
Spot Contracts	330,021	328,972	216,225	217,246
Forward Contracts	1,202,013	1,203,226	1,301,279	1,302,522
	2,548,110	2,549,723	2,547,339	2,549,825
Net Position (long) (b)	771			102
Swiss Franc ($250M)				
Ledger Accounts (c)	31,768	11,932	36,052	13,571
Spot Contracts	1,526	593	2,566	969
Forward Contracts	11,174	4,274	6,545	2,521
	44,468	16,799	45,163	17,061
Net Position (short) (d)			695	262

(a) Includes both forward purchases and sales and corresponding assets and liabilities. Excess liabilities over assets represents hedging of interest receivable.

(b) Split position caused by failure of bank to properly revalue its nostro accounts on a regular basis. Corrected during the examination.

(c) Does not include Swiss Franc 1,000M (US$ 386M) unhedged investment in a Swiss subsidiary and Swiss Franc 573M (US$ 217M) unhedged investment in branch fixed assets. Unhedged term "long" position approved by senior bank management.

(d) Net overnight position in excess of established limit. Formally approved as a special situation by senior management prior to the transaction.

Maturity Gaps. Exchange risk may exist, by virtue of maturity gaps, even though the bank has no net open position (assets equaling liabilities). Gaps are the result of unmatched forward maturities creating days or longer periods of uneven cash inflows and outflows. For example, a maturity spread of a bank's assets, liabilities, and future contracts may reflect a prolonged period over which substantial amounts of a particular currency will be received well in advance of any scheduled offsetting payments (positive gap). The bank must decide whether:

- To hold the currency in its nostro accounts.
- To invest or place it short-term.
- To sell it (spot or forward) for delivery at the time the gap begins and to repurchase it (spot or forward) for delivery at the time the gap ends.
- To use any combination of those alternatives.

The converse situation, wherein the maturity spread reflects maturing shorter-term liabilities or substantial cash outflows prior to maturities of offsetting assets (negative gap), obviously involves liquidity implications which do not exist in the positive gap. The bank must meet its obligations at maturity. Therefore, it must have the ability to borrow the currency short-term or be in a position to purchase (spot or forward) for delivery at the time the gap begins and, perhaps, sell (spot or forward) for delivery at the time the gap ends. The decision to close either gap when it is created, or leave it open until a later date, is determined by analyzing the money market interest rates, as well as the difference (the swap rate) between any applicable spot and forward, or two forward, exchange rates. The loss exposure, or profit potential, for the bank is measured by the anticipated, or actual, movement in the swap rate between the time the gap is created and the time it is closed. The interrelationship between interest rates and the swap rate as well as the conversion of the swap rate to an annual percentage rate and vice versa, are discussed in subsequent paragraphs. (Examples of maturity distribution schedules appropriate for use in preparing the report of examination appear below. Note that they balance to the open position schedules above.)

Maturity	Deutschemark		Swiss Franc		Canadian Dollar	
	Net	Cumulative	Net	Cumulative	Net	Cumulative
May 5	235	235	108	108	588	588
6	-200	35	-25	83	-36,591	-36,003
7	-11,639	-11,604	-722	-639	-35,295	-71,298
8		-11,604		-639	25,377	-45,921
9	5,384	-6,220	20,246	19,607	65,477	19,556
10		-6,220		19,607		19,556
11		-6,220		19,607		19,556
12	-41,111	-47,331 (a)	2,489	22,096	-65,959	-46,403
13	40,460	-6,871	-8,131	13,965	3,332	-43,071
14	15,108	8,237	-28,383 (b)	-14,418	13,350	-29,721
15	14,240	22,477		-14,157	-1,001	-30,722
16	2,260	20,217		-14,157	-272	-30,994
17		20,217		-14,157		-30,994
18		20,217		-14,157		-30,994
19	-1,824	18,393		-14,157	2,218	-28,776
20	-14,988	3,405	6,003	-8,154	35,589	6,813
21	37,770	41,175 (a)	15,920	7,766	4,190	11,003
22	-20,361	20,814	7,043	14,809	-4,930	6,813
23	3,015	23,829		14,809	-4,767	1,406
24		23,829		14,809		1,406
25		23,829		14,809		1,406
26		23,829		14,809		1,406
27	20,382	44,221	-24,477	-9,668	-34,562	-33,156
28	-11,600	32,621	-222	-9,890	10,041	-23,115
29		32,621		-9,890	3,075	-20,040
30	-82,367	-49,746 (a)	-3,783	-13,683	-39,935	-59,975
31		-49,746 (a)		-13,683		-59,975
June	17,653	-32,093	2,636	-11,047	37,578	-22,397
July	9,345	-22,748	6,141	-4,906 (b)	-27,599	-49,996
Aug	-3,209	-25,957	8,133	3,227	9,216	-40,780
Sept	22,504	-3,453	4,779	8,006	-32,125	-72,905
Oct	966	-2,487	-6,799	1,207	70,205	-2,700
Nov	-3,042	-5,529	5,640	6,847	-6,543	-9,243
Dec	13,266	7,737		6,847	-8,531	-17,774
19X1	-11,944	-4,207	-7,542	-695	21,582	3,808
19X2	800	-3,407			-941	2,894
19X3	858	-2,549			750	3,644
19X4					-2,617	1,027
After					-256	771
Summary:	Continuous cumulative negative gap from 5/30/XX to 9/30/XX, ascending to a high negative figure of DM72.71MM on 6/9/XX. (a)		Continuous cumulative negative gap from 5/27/XX to 8/13/XX, ascending to a high negative figure of SF27.7MM on 7/14/XX. (b)		Continuous cumulative negative gap from 5/27/XX to 11/17/XX, ascending to a high negative figure of C$77.6MM on 10/1/XX.	

(a) Cumulative maturity gap in excess of the DM 40,000M established limit. Corrected May 7, 19XX.
(b) Net daily maturity gap in excess of the SF 25,000M established limit. Special situation approved by senior

division management.

Although controlled and monitored by senior management, day-to-day supervision of net positions and maturity gaps is usually the responsibility of the foreign exchange and money market traders and, perhaps, a line supervisor. However, regardless of the care with which those functions are managed, factors beyond the direct control of bank officers affect liquidity and exposure to interest and exchange rate movement. Proper evaluation of such factors requires close coordination and effective communication among the trading, lending, correspondent relations, and economic research functions within the bank. Some such exposure factors may be identified as follows:

Customer Creditworthiness and Delivery Capabilities. In entering into any money market or foreign exchange transaction, the bank must be confident that the counterparty possesses the financial soundness and liquidity required to meet his or her obligations at maturity.

Money market assets expose the bank to credit risk on the entire amount of their face value. The liquidity considerations arising from the unanticipated non-repayment of those assets, particularly when proceeds are intended to meet maturing liabilities presumably in the same currency, should be obvious. The bank must satisfy its liability and again fund the asset, perhaps for an undetermined period and at a relatively unfavorable rate.

Foreign exchange transactions may involve the same liquidity and rate risks as money market transactions. However, the inherent credit risks are measured differently. Foreign exchange transactions are normally considered to be void of, or contain less than face value, credit risk except on the day(s) on which they are settled. For example, every foreign exchange transaction involves the exchange of one currency for another. If a counterparty is unable to deliver at maturity the currency that it has contracted to sell, the bank must either dispose of the currency it acquired for delivery under the contract or purchase the currency that it had expected to receive and had, in turn, contracted to deliver to a third party. If the bank had known in advance that the counterparty would default, its exchange risk exposure would have been determined by the difference between the contracted rates and the rates (spot or forward) at which funds could be obtained between the time it received prior warning and the maturity of the contract. Some bankers would attribute the rate difference to credit risk, although others would maintain that no credit risk existed prior to settlement date because there would be no need for funds to be paid or exchanged. However, of importance is the fact that the bank in that instance would not lose the full amount of the contract. If the bank had not received prior warning, the liquidity considerations could obviously be more severe. Also, the bank's exposure (depending on whether it had or had not transferred its payment prior to knowledge of default) would range from an exchange profit (less nostro overdraft charges relating to the sale contract to the third party) to a credit loss equal to the face amount of the defaulted contract. In that regard, credit (delivery) risk is considered to be more severe when the home country of one or both of the currencies being traded lies to the east of the bank. For example (assume the bank is selling a European currency for U.S. dollars), most European clearing mechanisms would not accept items for processing on the same day if they were received after 12 noon. Thus, to meet European clearing requirements on settlement (maturity) date, a United States bank must advise its European correspondent by cable on the previous business day to charge its account and credit the account of the counterparty. This is done without the United States bank's knowledge of whether the counterparty will advise (or be open for business to advise) its U.S. correspondent to make a similar transfer, e.g., to charge its account and credit that of the United States bank. If, in fact, the foreign bank does not advise its U.S. correspondent to make the transfer, the United States bank could lose the entire face amount of the contract. In summary, the credit risk is generally limited to the difference between the contracted rate and the prevailing spot rate except on maturity date when the possibility of delivery against nonreceipt of counterpart funds could result in a loss of the full face value of the contract.

Economic and Political Considerations. Political changes and/or adverse economic trends within a country are likely to be accompanied by shifts in policies which often affect such factors as interest rates, investment levels, capital flows, overall payments balances, and foreign exchange reserves. Such policies, whether based on economic necessity or changing attitudes, might affect the availability of exchange to counterparties or the bank's branches within the country or even the convertibility of that country's currency in other markets. In either case, the exchange rates for that currency will be subject to additional demand and supply considerations while sources of cover or liquidity in that currency may vanish.

Policy

The relative importance of each of those risk determinants varies with each currency traded and with the country of each counterparty. Senior bank management must fully understand the risks involved in foreign exchange and money market operations and must establish, in writing, its goals and policies regarding those risks. Management must be able to defend logically the basis upon which such policies are formed. It is imperative that responsible officers, traders, clerks, and auditors understand, without exception, the intent as well as the detail set forth in those directives.

At a minimum, policies should define dealing limits and reporting requirements as well as accounting, adequate audit and control systems to provide proper surveillance over those limits and exceptions thereto.

Limits must be established for overnight net positions in each currency. Depending on the size of the limits and the manner in which they are calculated, a smaller aggregate position limit for all currencies may be desirable. An aggregate limit should not permit the netting of short against long positions but should require that they be added to determine conformance to that limit. Many U.S. banks presently are considering daylight (intraday) position limits which are practical only if efficient computerization and input systems are in effect to incorporate each trade into the appropriate currency position at nearly the precise moment it is transacted. A common argument against intraday limits is that traders will only take those daylight positions they can cover by the end of the day. The solution to that argument might well lie in the frequency with which overnight position limits are exceeded and the reason for each excess position.

Gap (net inflow and outflow) limits must be instituted to control the risk of adverse rate movement and liquidity pressures for each currency per each daily, weekly, or bi-weekly future time frame designated in the bank's maturity reports. Such limits might range from stated absolute amounts per time frame to weighted limits which emphasize increasing rate movement exposure applicable to the relative distance into the future in which the gap appears.

Aggregate trading and placement limits must be established for each customer, based primarily on the amount of business considered to be appropriate to its creditworthiness and, secondly, on the volume of its foreign currency needs. In addition, absolute sub-limits should be placed upon the amount of that customer's business that may be settled on one day. Should the customer be unable to meet obligations on one day, the trader will:

- Be forewarned against delivery prior to receipt of customer funds on the remaining contracts outstanding, and
- Have an opportunity to determine whether alternate cover must be obtained to meet third party transactions that may initially have provided cover for remaining transactions with that customer.

Some argue that it is difficult to monitor aggregate volume limits effectively and nearly impossible to insure compliance with settlement limits for a large number of customers. Nevertheless, there is no excuse for the absence of an effective settlement limit program for at least those relationships that possess a greater potential for late delivery or default. In such instances, the bank should require counterparty transfer advices by cable rather than by mail.

Reports. Properly designed reports are the most important supervisory tool available to management. They must be prepared in a concise, uniform, and accurate manner and submitted punctually.

Management should receive daily net position reports for each applicable currency. Normally, position reports should include all foreign currency balance sheet items and future contracts as well as after-hour and holdover transactions, with the exception of fixed assets and equity investments. The hedging of those investments is usually a management decision outside the normal responsibility of the traders. The reports should be prepared by the foreign exchange and money market bookkeeping section and be reconciled daily to the trader's blotter. In the event that formal position reports cannot be submitted at the end of the applicable business day, management must at least be apprised of the trader's estimated position at the end of each day, particularly, before weekends and holidays.

Gap or maturity reports are essential to the proper management of a bank's liquidity in each foreign currency, and significant gaps may affect overall liquidity. Those reports should reflect daily gaps for at least the first 2 weeks to 1 month. Beyond that time, gap periods of a maximum of 2 weeks each are preferred. Gap reports, inherently, are accurate only for the day on which they are prepared. Therefore, it is essential that banks have the capability to produce detailed computerized reports daily. A variety of computerized management summaries can then be generated with ease. Loans, deposits, and future contracts as well as commitments to take or place deposits should be reflected in the periods in which they are scheduled for rollover or interest adjustment.

In most instances, an additional report reflecting those items at final maturity is desirable in analyzing the bank's medium and longer-term dependence on money market funding sources.

Exception reports must be generated immediately upon the creation of excesses, to position limits, gap limits, and customer trading and settlement limits. Excesses over any established limits should conform to overall policy guidelines and should receive prior approval by the responsible supervisory officers. If prior approval is not possible, evidence of subsequent supervisor concurrence or disagreement as well as any corrective action should be available for audit review and management records.

Revaluation and Accounting Systems. Such systems should accurately determine actual as well as estimated future profits and losses and present them in such a manner as to facilitate proper income analysis by management, bank supervisory personnel, and the public. One system widely used by banks is illustrated below. This system is capable of presenting separately, each of the following:

- Actual realized profit or loss as determined by applying current spot rates to balance sheet accounts as well as contracts of very near maturities. Adjustments to the local currency book values would either be allocated and posted to each of the applicable local currency ledger accounts or, for short interim periods, be charged to a separate "foreign exchange adjustment" account with an offset to P&L.

- Unrealized (estimated future) profit or loss on future transactions as determined by applying the appropriate forward rates to the net positions reflected for each future period appearing in the bank's gap or maturity reports. An "estimated profit (loss) on foreign exchange—futures" account would be charged for the amount of the adjustment with an offset to P&L. Provided that the amount of that adjustment is the difference between the existing forward rates and the actual contract rates, each month's entries merely involve reversing the adjustment from the prior revaluation and submitting the new figures.

The previous discussion may be more clearly understood when read in conjunction with the typical bank revaluation worksheet below. The illustration reflects a revaluation of the Deutschemark position above.

- As discussed in subsequent paragraphs entitled Financial Swaps and Arbitrage, simultaneously contracted spot purchase and future sale transactions performed to acquire foreign currency funds for temporary loan or investment purposes should be segregated from regular trading activities when determining revaluation profits or losses. Those "swap" profits (discounts) or costs (premiums), as determined by the difference in local currency value between the two contracted rates, are fixed. They are locked-in at the time the forward side of the swap is completed. They should be amortized or accreted over the life of the swap and must be properly allocated to reflect the true yield on the particular investment for which the swap was entered and the real income from loans and securities.

Revaluation Worksheet
May 4, 19XX
(amounts in thousands)

Deutschemark	Assets	Liabilities	Net Position	Rate	Market Value	Book Value	Profit or Loss	
Ledger Accounts	563,437	645,013	-81,576	.39155	-31,941	-34,849	+2,908	(a)
Spot Contracts	23,502	15,973	+7,529	.39155	+2,948	+3,093	-145	(a)
Forward Contracts Dec. 21 to Jan. 20	0	56,926	-56,926	.39230	-22,332	-21,986	-346	(b)
Jan. 21 to Feb. 20	100,415	111,420	-11,005	.39335	-4,328	-4,328	0	(b)
Feb. 21 to Mar. 20	56,246	49,457	+6,789	.38795	+2,635	+2,578	+57	(b)
Mar. 21 to Apr. 20	0	0	0		0	0	0	(b)
Apr. 21 to May 20	203,717	200,315	+3,402	.38810	+1,320	-177	+1,497	(b)
May 21 to Jun. 20	0	0	0		0	0	0	(b)
Jun. 21 to Jul. 20	98,426	0	+98,426	.38825	+37,648	+37,117	+531	(b)
Jul. 21 to Aug. 20	301,226	295,556	+5,670	.38830	+2,202	+2,475	-273	(b)
Aug. 21 to Sep. 20	37,427	39,256	-1,829	.39350	-718	+2,547	-3,265	(b)
Sep. 21 to Oct. 20	0	0	0		0	0	0	(b)
Oct. 21 to Nov. 20	222,705	185,716	+36,989	.38875	+14,379	+16,413	-2,034	(b)
Nov. 21 to Dec. 20	0	0	0		0	0	0	(b)
Dec. 21 and over	10,000	20,018	-10,018	.39420	-3,949	-3,956	+7	(b)
Total	1,617,101	1,619,650	-2,549		-2,136	-1,073	-1,063	(b)

(a) Allocated to appropriate balance sheet accounts with offset to P&L.
(b) Allocated as credit to unrealized loss account and debit to P&L.

The Financial Accounting Standards Board's (FASB) Statement of Financial Accounting Standards No. 8 prescribes a different approach to portfolio valuation than that previously described. The principles and procedures set forth in that statement are outlined as follows:

- Balance sheet accounts denominated in foreign currencies should be translated and revalued using the following rates:

Foreign currency on hand	Spot
Due from banks (nostro accounts)	Spot
Investments in debt instruments	Spot
Equity Investments:	
Carried at cost	Historical
Carried at current market price	Spot
Loans and accrued interest receivable	Spot
Bank premises and equipment	Historical
Deposits, borrowings, and accrued interest payable	Spot

- Forward exchange contracts should be revalued using the following rates:

Contracts that are part of a financial swap transaction or otherwise used to hedge balance sheet accounts, such as loans or deposits	Spot
Contracts that are not categorized above	Appropriate forward rate

- Gains and losses, whether realized or unrealized, resulting from revaluations of foreign currency transactions should be recorded as income and expense. However, discounts and premiums on forward exchange contracts that are part of financial swap transactions should be amortized (accreted) to income over the life of the swap and should be considered as an adjustment of the interest factor.

In analyzing both methods, at least one significant difference is apparent. The FASB method requires that financial swap related assets, liabilities, and future contracts be revalued at spot rates so that those assets and liabilities may be reflected in the balance sheet at their current market values. As a result, the local currency carrying values of those assets and liabilities would be adjusted, at each revaluation, to values that would normally differ from their already contracted liquidation values.

Analysis of the revaluation working papers generated by either method should permit the same convenient approaches to evaluation of earnings and identification of accruing losses in the forward book as are described in step 17 of the examination procedures in this section. It is conceivable, however, that this convenience could be lost in a fully computerized revaluation system using the FASB method.

Departmental Organization and Control. It is imperative that there be a distinct separation of duties and responsibilities between the trading and the accounting and confirmation functions within the department. The many opportunities for greater bank profit or personal financial gain, whether by speculating beyond loosely controlled limits, concealing contracts because of poor confirmation procedures, or by simple fraud, may be too tempting even to the most trusted employees. Periodic audits and examinations are no substitute for sound continuing safeguards, and the numerous guidelines in the Internal Control Questionnaire in this section cannot be overemphasized.

Supervision of Branches and Subsidiaries. Whether a bank maintains central control over all foreign exchange and money market activities at the head office or elects to decentralize that control, the policies, systems, internal controls, and reporting procedures should not differ among separate offices within the bank.

In either case, the bank should be apprised of its worldwide positions by daily summary reports. Detailed net position and maturity gap reports should be received periodically in order to prepare consolidations, as required, and to monitor individual unit trading volume and funding methods. Information provided in the Treasury Department monthly foreign currency reports is adequate for the preparation of reports of examination and can be adapted easily to reporting for currencies other than those specified in the reporting instructions.

Federal Financial Institutions Examination Council Uniform Guideline. The OCC adopted the "Uniform Guideline on Internal Control for Foreign Exchange in Commercial Banks" on June 11, 1980. This guideline establishes minimum standards for documentation, accounting, and auditing for foreign exchange operations of banks supervised by the OCC, the Federal Deposit Insurance Corporation, and the Federal Reserve System. The minimum standards adopted either have been incorporated into the Foreign Exchange Internal Control Questionnaire or are already included in the Handbook sections on Internal Control, Internal and External Audits, and Working Papers.

The Market

Banks may fund their foreign currency activities through either money market transactions or foreign exchange transactions, or both. Money market instruments exist in a variety of forms and under a number of different names. However, each of them can be categorized as a type of deposit, loan, or borrowing and are all specifically covered in other sections of this handbook. Therefore, only market considerations most applicable to foreign exchange are discussed here.

Spot Exchange. Although the spot market typically refers to the purchase or sale of foreign exchange for delivery in 2 business days, many U.S. banks consider transactions maturing in as many as 10 business days as spot exchange. The latter definition is used generally to facilitate revaluation accounting policies and to initiate final confirmation and settlement verification procedures on future contracts nearing maturity.

The spot rate for any particular currency might be determined strictly by the bid and offered rates at which the central bank of that country will officially trade. It might be pegged to another currency or group of currencies or allowed to float freely in accordance with supply and demand. However, the rate may change at any time based on many overriding economic, political, or market factors.

Forward Exchange. Future exchange contracts are typically made for delivery in 1, 2, 3, and 6 months, i.e., actual deliveries are made in exactly the stated number of months from the normal spot date. In most major currencies, however, contracts can be made for "odd dates" or in the exact number of days desired by the counterparty. "Odd date" rates can generally be determined by interpolation between spot and forward rates or between two forward rates.

Forward exchange rates usually are quoted in terms of their premium or discount over spot. Though they move with fluctuations in the spot rate, the amount of the premium or discount (the swap rate) is determined by the net accessible interest rate differential existing between the two countries, e.g., the difference in interest rate levels further adjusted for reserve requirements and other cost factors. The currency of the country in which interest rates are higher will sell at a forward discount relative to the currency of the lower interest rate and vice versa. For example, if the net accessible interest rate in a country were higher by 3 percent per annum than that in the United States, and the spot rate for that currency was U.S. $2.4000, then the forward discount normally would be $.0720 per year (2.4000 x .03), or $.0060 per month. Should the forward discount move from the 60 points per month, there will immediately be an opportunity for arbitrage through a financial swap.

Financial Swaps. A financial swap is the combination of a spot purchase or sale against a forward sale or purchase of one currency in exchange for another. It is merely trading one currency (lending) for another currency (borrowing) for that period of time between which the spot exchange is made and the forward contract matures. The swap is the simple identification of one transaction contracted at the spot rate with another contracted at the forward rate to establish the exchange cost or profit related to the temporary movement of funds into another currency and back again. That exchange (swap) profit or cost must then be applied to the rate of interest earned on the loan or investment for which the exchange was used. For example, the true yield of an investment for 90 days in United Kingdom Treasury bills cannot be determined without having considered the cost or profit resulting from the swap needed to make pounds sterling available for that investment. By the same token, the true trading profits or losses generated by the trader cannot be determined if financial swap profits and expenses are charged to the exchange function rather than being allocated to the department whose loans or investments the swap actually funded.

Arbitrage. As it pertains to money markets and foreign exchange, arbitrage may take several forms. The creation of an open position in a currency in anticipation of a favorable future movement in the exchange rate, in addition to being speculative, is sometimes referred to as arbitrage in time. Buying a currency in one market and simultaneously selling it for a profit in another market is called arbitrage in space. Slightly more complicated is the practice of interest arbitrage that involves the movement of fund from one currency to another so they may be invested at a higher yield. The real yield advantage in such a situation is not determined merely by the difference in interest rates between the two investment choices, but rather, by subtracting the cost of transferring funds into the desired currency and back again (the swap cost) from the interest differential. For example, in the situation described under Forward Exchange, there is no arbitrage incentive involved in "swapping" from dollars into the other currency at a 60 point per month discount (swap cost) which exactly offsets the 3 percent gain in interest. However, should the swap rate move to 40 points per month (or 480 points per year), the investment might become attractive. This can easily be tested by converting the swap rate to an annual percentage rate

$$\frac{\text{Discount or Premium} \times 360 \times 100}{\text{Spot rate} \times \text{No. of days of future contract}} \quad = \quad \% \text{ P.A.}$$

$$\frac{.0040 \times 360 \times 100}{2.4000 \times 30} \quad = \quad 2\% \text{ P.A.}$$

which results in a true yield incentive of 1 percent, 3 percent less the swap cost of 2 percent.

As discussed earlier, unless the bank's accounting system can identify swap costs or profits and allocate them to the investments for which they were entered, both the earnings on those investments and the earnings upon which the trader's performance are measured will be misstated.

Options. Option contracts permit a bank to contract to buy from or sell to a customer when that customer can only generally predict the dates between which he or she must trade. The option contract specifies both dates, and the rate cited is that which in the judgement of the trader at the time of making the contract contains the least exposure for the bank. That type of contract is commonly requested by commercial customers wishing to cover drafts drawn under letters of credit denominated in foreign currency. Such contracts are always risky since there is no way for the bank to acquire a precisely matching cover.

Compensated Contracts. There are occasions when both parties are agreeable to altering the terms of an existing contract. Such alterations should be approved by an impartial bank officer. Operations personnel must be advised of each compromise to avoid settlement in accordance with the original instructions and terms.

Foreign exchange and money markets do not merely exist but must be created by parties who are willing to engage in commercial and financial transactions proposed to them by others. If a bank wishes to solicit such business, it must be prepared to quote bid and offered rates of exchange or interest for a given time period. The party requesting the rates has the option to buy or sell, deposit or borrow, at the stated rates or decline to deal. If the quoting bank prefers only to service its commercial customer's needs and otherwise remain relatively inactive, it will have to acquire cover for those transactions at another party's bid and offered rates compared to an active bank that has the advantage of dealing more frequently at its own rates. In addition, active market participation may enhance a bank's ability to borrow. It is important that those factors be considered in evaluating a bank's trading volume and liquidity.

1. Complete or update the Foreign Exchange section of the Internal Control Questionnaire.

2. Based upon the evaluation or internal controls and the work performed by internal and external auditors (see separate program), ascertain the scope of examination.

3. Test for compliance with policies, practices, procedures, and internal controls in conjunction with the remaining examination procedures. Also, obtain a listing of any deficiencies noted in the latest review done by internal/external auditors from the examiner assigned "Internal and External Audits," and determine if appropriate corrections have been made.

4. Perform appropriate verification procedures.

5. Obtain a trial balance, including local currency book values, of customer spot and future contract liabilities by customer and by maturity, and:

    a. Agree or reconcile balances to appropriate subsidiary controls and to the general ledger.

    b. Review reconciling items for reasonableness.

6. Using the appropriate sampling technique, select customers for examination. If verification procedures have been performed, use the same sample. (Refer to step 20 before performing steps 7 through 19.)

7. Prepare credit line sheets to include details below:

    a. Customer's aggregate foreign exchange liability in local currency equivalents.

    b. Customer's assigned trading volume limit.

    c. Transcribe book value equivalents of individual contracts (from the

---

trial balance obtained at step 5) in maturity order, indicating the foreign currency amount of each. If contracts are voluminous, summarize transcription to include:

- The average book value per contract.
- The combined book value amount, purchases plus sales, and date of the largest single day's settlement.
- The longest outstanding maturity.
- The total of all future contracts in each foreign currency.

    d. Customer's assigned daily settlement limit.

    e. Frequency of recent overdrafts in current account and, if possible, whatever reasonable identification can be made to late delivery of prior foreign exchange contract maturities.

    f. Past compliance with trading volume and settlement limits as determined from review of liability ledger record.

8. Identify those contracts with counterparties who are affiliates of or otherwise related to the bank, its directors, officers, employees, or major shareholders, and:

    a. Compare the contracted rates with available rates for the same transaction date or with other contracts entered as of the same transaction date for the same tenor.

    b. Investigate any instances involving off-market rates.

9. Obtain from the examiner assigned "International Loan Portfolio Management" the schedules on the following if they are applicable to the foreign exchange area:

    a. Delinquencies.

    b. Shared national credits.

    c. Interagency Country Exposure Review Committee credits.

d. Previously criticized loans (internally or by examiners).

e. Information on directors, executive officers, principal shareholders, and their interests.

f. Any useful information resulting from the review of the minutes of the foreign exchange and money market committee or any similar committee.

g. Reports furnished to the foreign exchange and money management committee or any similar committee.

h. Reports furnished to the board of directors.

i. A list of affiliated companies.

10. Transcribe or compare information from the above schedules to credit line sheets, where appropriate.

11. Prepare credit line sheets for any foreign exchange customer not in the sample which, based on information derived from the above, requires in-depth review.

12. Obtain liability and other information on common borrowers from examiners assigned to cash items, overdrafts, and loan areas, and, together, decide who will review the customer relationships. Pass or retain completed credit line sheets.

13. Analyze each customer relationship considering the guidelines set forth in the international sections, as they pertain to:

a. Commercial loans for private and commercial counterparties.

b. Due from foreign banks—time for banking and financial counterparties.

(Generally, a customer's obligation to the bank under foreign exchange contracts would not be classified. However, if a customer's financial condition is so severe, i.e., doubtful or loss, that its ability to meet its foreign exchange commitments is questionable, the combined book value of contracts, purchases plus sales, representing the largest single day's settlement should be appropriately criticized or classified.)

14. Review the most readily available record and/or source of spot exchange rate movement vis-a-vis the local currency to determine which currencies, if any, have experienced a substantial degree to appreciation or depreciation over the recent past. (Give particular attention, in step 13, to the creditworthiness of those counterparties who have contracted either to deliver appreciating currencies to, or purchase depreciating currencies from, the bank. In the event of non-performance by a counterparty that has agreed to (a) deliver an appreciating currency, the bank's cost to cover any offsetting sales contracts might be substantial, or (b) purchase a depreciating currency, the bank might be forced to sell the currency it had acquired for delivery at a substantial loss. As one source for identifying such currencies, each monthly Federal Reserve Bulletin provides a history of annual and monthly averages of certified noon buying rates in New York for cable transfers.)

15. Obtain or prepare the following data (separately for each foreign currency involved, and to include book value equivalents), as of the examination date, to be used in performing subsequent examination steps:

    a. A list of subsidiary control ledger totals for all balance sheet and memoranda general ledger accounts by account number and/or title.

    b. A trial balance of all balance sheet asset and liability items by maturity.

    c. A trial balance of all spot and future exchange contracts by maturity.

    d. Copies of the trader's daily position sheets and/or reports.

    e. Copies of the accounting department's daily position sheets and/or reports and reconcilements to the trader's positions.

    f. If not included in copies obtained under d and e, a detailed listing of all holdover and after-hour transactions.

g. If not available as of examination date, copies of the accounting department's last maturity gap reports. (After analysis has been performed, pass maturity gap reports, to include appropriate local currency equivalents, to the "Funds Management" examiner.)

h. If not prepared as of examination date, copies of the last revaluation worksheets.

i. All limit exception reports.

16. Prepare examination report net position and maturity schedules, and:

(Commitments to take or place foreign currency deposits must be included in the maturity schedules in order that all anticipated cash inflows and outflows are properly reflected. However, those items should not be included in the net position schedules other than in footnote form.)

a. Compare results to bank prepared net position and maturity gap reports, if available for the same date.

- Footnote any material differences.
- Explain any deficiencies.

b. Compare results to established limits, and review exception approvals thereto.

17. Check the most recent revaluation working papers and resultant accounting entries to determine that:

a. Foreign currency amounts and book values were properly reconciled to subsidiary ledger controls.

b. Rates used are representative of market rates as of revaluation date, and

- If obtained from the traders, that they have been verified with independent sources. (Daily, 10:00 AM, mid-point, spot and future, New York interbank market rates for commonly traded currencies are available as needed at each regional office or the

International Banking Activity Examinations, Washington, D.C.)

   c. Arithmetic is correct.

   d. Profit and loss results are separately recorded and reported to management for:

- Realized profit or loss, i.e., that which is determined through the application of spot rates.
- Unrealized (estimated future) profit and loss, i.e., that which is determined through the application of forward rates.

   e. Financial swap related assets, liabilities, and future contracts are excluded from the normal revaluation process so that the results identified in d. reflect more accurately the trader's outright dealing performance.

   f. Financial swap related costs and profits are:

- Amortized over the life of the applicable swap.
- Appropriately accounted for as interest income and expense on loans, securities, etc.

18. Review working papers for selected revaluations performed since last examination, and test check as in step 17 above, and, if satisfied that they are accurate:

   a. Analyze combined realized earnings to determine that profits are commensurate with risks taken.

   b. Analyze monthly unrealized revaluation results (forecasts) to determine that:

- The resulting amount for the last revaluation, if a loss, is not large.
- An increasing loss trend over previous revaluations does not exist. (Although month-to-month variations are not uncommon, an increasing unrealized loss trend could indicate that a trader is caught in a loss position and is pursuing a notion that a negative trend in the exchange rate for that currency will reverse and, if

combined with an ever multiplying increase in his or her volume, might eventually repay his or her accumulated losses.)

19. Review the confirmation discrepancy log, and observe the confirmation process to determine:

    a. That incoming confirmations are delivered directly to the confirmation clerk and that:

       • Discrepancies are recorded.
       • Discrepancies are reported to an appropriate officer and are resolved promptly.

    b. That outgoing confirmations are processed in compliance with policies governing:

       • Initial procedures.
       • Follow-up procedures.
       • The level of involvement by internal auditors in follow-up procedures.

    c. If the confirmation discrepancy log discloses counterparties which:

       • Are often or consistently slow in confirming.
       • Often or consistently make errors in confirmation preparation.

20. Determine compliance with laws, regulations, and rulings pertaining to foreign exchange activities by performing the following for:

    a. 12 CFR 20.5 — Monthly Consolidated Foreign Currency Report of Banks and Federal Branches — Form FFIEC 035:

       • Review for accuracy the most recently prepared monthly report.
       • Select random bank prepared net position reports, and determine whether they are being filed as required and are accurate. (Be alert to instances in which net positions are generally large but reduced as of the month-end reporting dates.)

21. Discuss with appropriate officer(s), and prepare appropriate report summaries of:

a. Net position schedules.

b. Maturity gap schedules.

c. Frequent or sizeable excesses over any established limits.

d. Any limits deemed excessive relative to:

- Management's policy goals regarding the nature and volume of business intended.
- The bank's capital structure.
- The creditworthiness of trading counterparties.
- Individual currencies for which limited spot and future markets exist.
- Experience of traders.
- The bank's foreign exchange earnings record.

e. The absence of any limits deemed appropriate in present and foreseeable circumstances.

f. Customers whose obligations are otherwise previously classified or intended to be criticized.

g. Foreign exchange contracts which, for any other reason, are questionable in quality or ultimate settlement.

h. Violations of laws, regulations, or rulings.

i. Deficiencies in internal controls.

j. Other matters regarding efficiency and general condition of the foreign exchange department.

22. Prepare a memorandum, and update the work program with any information that will facilitate future examinations.

Foreign Exchange
(Section 813)   Internal Control Questionnaire

Review the bank's internal controls, policies, practices, and procedures regarding foreign exchange trading. The bank's systems should be documented in a complete and concise manner and include, where appropriate, narrative descriptions, flowcharts, copies of forms used, and other pertinent information. Items marked with asterisks require substantiation by observation or testing.

Policies

1.   Has the board of directors, consistent with its responsibilities, adopted written policies governing:

   a. Trading limits, including:

   - Overall trading volume?
   - Overnight net position limits per currency?
   - Intra-day net position limit per currency?
   - Aggregate net position limit for all currencies combined?
   - Maturity gap limits per currency?
   - Individual customer aggregate trading limits, including spot transactions?
   - Written approval of excesses to above limits?

   b. Segregation of duties among traders, bookkeepers, and confirmation personnel?

   c. Accounting and revaluation procedures?

   d. Management reporting requirements?

2.   Do policies attempt to minimize:

   a. Undue pressure on traders to meet specific budgeted earnings goals?

   b. Undue pressure on traders, by account officers, to provide preferred rates to certain customers?

3.   Are traders prohibited from dealing with customers for whom trading lines have not been established?*

4.   Are all personnel, except perhaps the head trader, prohibited from effecting transactions via off-premises communication facilities?

5.   Is approval by a non-trading officer required for all compensated transactions?

6.   Do credit approval procedures exist for settlement (delivery) risk either in the form of settlement limits or other specific management controls?

7.   Does a policy procedure exist to insure that, in the event of an uncertain or emergency situation, the bank's delivery will not be made prior to receipt of counterpart funds?

8.   Do the above policies apply to all branch offices as well as majority-owned or controlled subsidiaries of the bank?

9.   Does the bank have written policies covering:

     a. Foreign exchange transactions with its own employees?

     b. Foreign exchange transactions with members of its board of directors?

     c. Its traders' personal foreign exchange activities?

     d. Its employees' personal business relationships with foreign exchange and money brokers with whom the bank trades?

10. Are the above policies understood and uniformly interpreted by all traders as well as accounting and auditing personnel?*

Trading Function

11. Is a trader's position sheet maintained for each currency traded?

12. Is a trader's position report received by management at the end of each

trading day?*

13. Does the trader's position report reflect the same day's holdover and after-hours transactions?*

14. Are trader's dealing tickets pre-numbered?

    a. If so, are records and controls adequate to ascertain their proper sequential and authorized use?

    b. Regardless of whether or not pre-numbered,*

       • Are dealing tickets time date stamped, as completed, or
       • Are dealing tickets otherwise identified with the number of the resultant contract to provide a proper audit trail?

Accounting and Reporting

15. Is there a definite segregation of duties, responsibility, and authority between the trading room and the accounting and reporting functions within the division and/or branch?*

16. Are contract forms pre-numbered (if so, are records and controls adequate to insure their proper sequential and authorized use)?

17. Are contracts signed by personnel other than the traders?

18. Are after-hours or holdover contracts posted as of the dates contracted?*

19. Do accounting personnel prepare a daily position report, for each applicable currency, from the bank's general ledger, and:*

    a. Do reports include all accounts denominated in foreign currency?

    b. Are those reports reconciled daily to the trader's position report?

    c. Are identified or unreconciled differences reported immediately to management and to the head trader?

    d. Are all counterparty non-deliveries on expected settlements reported immediately to management and to the head trader?

20. Are maturity gap reports prepared for liquidity and foreign exchange managers at least bi-weekly to include:*

   a. Loans and deposits reflected in the appropriate forward maturity periods along with foreign exchange contracts?

   b. Loans, deposits, and foreign exchange contracts (specify whether reflected in the maturity periods in which they fall due or in which they are scheduled for rollover _____)?

   c. Commitments to accept or place deposits reflected in the appropriate maturity periods by both value and maturity dates?

   d. All those items (specify whether as of the day on which they mature or bi-weekly or monthly maturity periods _____)?

   e. All those items as of the day on which they mature, if necessary, i.e., in the event of a severe liquidity situation?

21. Does the accounting system render excesses of all limits identified at step 1 immediately to appropriate management, and is officer approval required?*

22. Are local currency equivalent subsidiary records for foreign exchange contracts balanced daily to the appropriate general ledger account(s)?*

23. Are foreign exchange record copy and customer liability ledger trial balances prepared and reconciled monthly to subsidiary control accounts by employees who do not process or record foreign exchange transactions?*

24. Do the accounting and filing systems provide for easy identification of "financial swap" related assets, liabilities, and future contracts by stamping contracts or maintaining a control register?

Confirmations

25. Is there a designated "confirmation clerk" within the accounting section of the division or branch?

   a. Incoming Confirmations:*

- Are incoming confirmations delivered directly to the confirmation clerk and not to trading personnel?
- Are signatures on incoming confirmations verified with signature cards for:
  - Authenticity?
  - Compliance with advised signatory authorizations of the counterparty?
- Are all data on each incoming confirmation verified with file copies of contracts to include:
  - Name?
  - Currency denomination and amount?
  - Rate?
  - Transaction date?
  - Preparation date, if different from transaction date?
  - Maturity date?
  - Delivery instructions, if applicable?
- Are discrepancies directed to an officer apart from the trading function for resolution?
- Is a confirmation discrepancy log or other record maintained to reflect the identity and disposition of each discrepancy?
- Are telex tapes retained for at least 90 days as ready reference to rates and delivery instructions?

   b. Outgoing Confirmations:*

- Are outgoing confirmations mailed/telexed on the day during which each trade is effected?
- Are outgoing confirmations addressed to the attention of persons other than trading personnel at counterparty locations?
- Does the accounting and/or filing system adequately segregate and/or identify booked contracts for which no incoming confirmations have been received?
- Are follow-up confirmations sent by the confirmation clerk if no corresponding, incoming confirmation is received within a limited

number of days after the contract is effected (if so, specify
_____)?

- Is involvement by the auditing department required if no
  confirmation is received within a limited number of days after the
  transmittal of the second request referred to above (if so, specify
  _____)?
- Are confirmation forms sent in duplicate to customers who do not
  normally confirm?
- Are return copies required to be signed?

Revaluations

26. Are revaluations of foreign currency accounts performed at least
    monthly?*

    a. Does the revaluation system provide for segregation of and separate
       accounting for:

       - Realized profits and losses, i.e., those which are determined
         through the application of spot rates?
       - Unrealized profits and losses, i.e., those which are determined
         through the application of forward rates?

    b. Are financial swap related assets, liabilities, and future contracts
       excluded from the revaluation process so that the results identified in
       a. above more accurately reflect the trader's outright dealing
       performance?

    c. Are financial swap costs and profits:

       - Amortized over the life of the applicable swap?
       - Appropriately accounted for as interest income and expense on
         loans, securities, etc?

    d. Are rates provided by, or at least verified with, sources other than the
       traders?

    Other

27. Is the bank's system capable of adequately disclosing sudden increases in trading volume by any one trader?*

28. Do such increases require officer review to insure that the trader is not doubling volume in an attempt to regain losses in his or her positions?

29. Does the bank retain information on, and authorizations for, all overdraft charges and brokerage bills within the last 12 months?

30. Does an appropriate officer review a comparison of brokerage charges, monthly, to determine if an inordinate share of the bank's business is directed to or handled by one broker?

Conclusion

31. Is the foregoing information an adequate basis for evaluating internal control in that there are no significant additional internal auditing procedures, accounting controls, administrative controls, or other circumstances that impair any controls or mitigate any weaknesses indicated above (explain negative answers briefly, and indicate conclusions as to their effect on specific examination or verification procedures)?

32. Based on a composite evaluation, as evidenced by answers to the foregoing questions, internal control is considered _____ (good, medium, or bad).

Verification Procedures

1. Obtain control of all outstanding contracts and number them sequentially so that they may be returned to the bank in the order in which they were received, and:

    a. Arrange them by currency for preparation of position worksheets for proof to or comparison with:

        - Foreign currency subsidiary ledgers.
        - The general ledger.
        - The bank's position report as of the same date.
        - Net position limits.
        - Aggregate trading limits.

    b. Arrange them by currency and by maturity for preparation of maturity worksheets and for comparison with the bank's maturity gap reports, if available, as of the same date, and check for compliance with gap limits.

    c. Arrange them by customer and by maturity, and:

        - Provide to customer liability ledgers.
        - Check for compliance with customer trading limits.
        - Check for compliance with customer settlement limits.

    d. Test for compliance with other limits, as appropriate.

2. Identify those contracts for which incoming confirmations have not yet been received as well as those for which incoming confirmations bear unresolved discrepancies.

    a. Unless bank personnel have taken follow-up action too recently to expect response, prepare and mail confirmation forms to include:

        - Counterparty name.

- Currency denominations and amounts.
- Rate.
- Transaction date.
- Maturity date.
- Settlement instructions, if applicable.

3. Using appropriate sampling techniques, select accounts from the trial balance, and perform the following:

   a. Prepare and mail confirmation forms to include the same information cited in 2a.

   b. After a reasonable time, mail second requests.

   c. Follow-up on any no-replies or exceptions, and resolve differences. Confirmation forms and return envelopes should be prepared:

      - By bank staff under examiner supervision.
      - On bank letterhead and signed by the auditor.
      - Using the bank's return address with conspicuous markings to insure their direct routing to the responsible examiner.

4. In conjunction with the audit staff, intercept at the bank's mail room all incoming confirmations for a period of several days to determine:

   a. If any contracts have been made but not booked.

   b. Extent to which the confirmation clerk, or other personnel, relies upon traders to resolve discrepancies.